CLOTHING

Peggy J. Parks

BLACKBIRCH PRESS

An imprint of Thomson Gale, a part of The Thomson Corporation

Detroit • New York • San Francisco • San Diego • New Haven, Conn. • Waterville, Maine • London • Munich

Picture Credits: Cover: Corel (top), © Giuseppe Aresu/Bloomberg News/Landov (bottom); © Art Today, Inc., 20, 21 (top), 30, 31; Courtesy of Bellarmine College, 11; © Bettmann/CORBIS, 4, 19, 25; © Burstein Collection/CORBIS, 6 (left column); © Pierre Colombel/CORBIS, 10 (top); Corel, 7; © Denver Public Library, 15; © Jay Dickman/CORBIS, 28; Courtesy of Dinkum Technology, 9 (top); Courtesy of Dr. Fred Fishel, 13 (inset); © Werner Forman/CORBIS, 10 (below); © Giasanti Gianni/CORBIS SYGMA, 5 (both); © Giraudon/Art Resource, NY, 8; © Dr. Dennis Kunkel/Visuals Unlimited, 13 (below); © Erich Lessing/Art Resource, NY, 6 (bottom right); Library of Congress, 17 (bottom), 18, 21 (bottom), 22, 23, 24; NASA, 26 (both), 27; © The Newark Museum/Art Resource, NY, 9; © Michael Nicholson/CORBIS, 17 (top); © North Wind Picture Archives, 14, 16; © Reuters/CORBIS, 29; © Swim Ink/CORBIS, 12

LIBRARY OF CONGRESS CATALOGING-IN-PUBLICATION DATA

Parks, Peggy, 1951-
 Clothing / Peggy J. Parks.
  p. cm. — (Yesterday and today)
 Includes bibliographical references and index.
 ISBN 1-56711-828-3 (hard cover : alk. paper)

Table of Contents

Ancient peoples wore clothing made of fur and animal skins for protection and warmth.

The First Clothing

The clothing worn in ancient times was simple, practical, and functional. In areas where the climate was warm, people wore very little clothing—and sometimes they wore no clothing at all. According to anthropologists (scientists who study the history of humans), nudity was common in ancient times. Some people may have started wearing clothes to cover their nakedness. Where climates were colder, humans dressed to protect themselves from the elements.

A group of anthropologists from Germany performed a study to determine when humans first began wearing clothes. They examined body lice, which are insects that make their home and lay their eggs in worn clothing. Body lice did not exist until people began to wear clothes. By studying the evolution of these insects, the scientists concluded that people started wearing clothes about seventy thousand years ago.

Unlike stones, shells, metal, and other remnants of ancient human behavior, clothing is too fragile to survive for tens of thousands of years. Without such physical evidence, anthropologists can only theorize about what humans wore in ancient times. They believe the first clothing was likely made from animal skins and furs, or from leaves and grass.

Ancient peoples sewed materials together to make basic garments such as capes, loincloths, or hooded parkas. They used crude sewing needles with thin pieces of animal tendon (called sinew) for thread. Ancient sewing needles made of bone and animal horn have been found buried in China as well as in other sites throughout Asia and Europe.

Ancient humans wore clothing for reasons that were very different from those of people today. Their clothes were meant to be functional and protective rather than stylish or fashionable.

The Iceman

In 1991, the frozen body of a man was discovered on a mountain in the Italian Alps. Anthropologists determined that the body was about five thousand years old, and they gave it a name—Ötzi the Iceman. Ötzi was clothed in a leather cape, loincloth, leggings, leather shoes, and a fur cap, as well as an outer garment made of grass. His garments were clearly functional—designed to protect him from the elements.

A scientist examines the five-thousand-year-old body of Ötzi the Iceman. Ötzi was discovered dressed in leather clothing (inset), which protected him from the weather.

Prehistory

500 B.C.

100 B.C.

A.D. 100

200

500

1000

1200

1300

1400

1500

1600

1700

1800

1900

2000

2100

Weaving and Spinning

In ancient times, humans made clothing out of animal skins because that was the only material with which they were familiar. Beginning about 8000 B.C., people learned how to make fabric from plants. Ancient Egyptians used flax (a flowering plant) to make a cloth called linen. They soaked the plant stems in water to separate the fibers; then they beat the fibers to soften them. The next steps were to spin the fibers into thread and weave the thread to make fabric. The fabric was either woven by hand or with crude weaving machines called looms. Linen was used to make simple clothing, such as shirts for men and dresses for women. Linen fabric was lightweight, so it was ideal for people living in the hot Egyptian climate.

Around 5000 B.C., people in Asia and Europe discovered that fabric could be made from wool. They raised sheep, cut the wool off the animals' bodies, and combed it out. The last steps were to spin the fibers into thread and weave the fabric. The wool contained a fatty substance called lanolin, so wool fabric was water-resistant as well as warm. Wool was used for many types of clothing, including socks, hats, and capes. In the Middle East, people sometimes beat raw wool into a matted fabric called felt, which they used to make different types of garments.

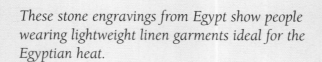

These stone engravings from Egypt show people wearing lightweight linen garments ideal for the Egyptian heat.

6

This modern Indian woman wears the brightly colored cotton fabric that has been made in her country for thousands of years.

Prehistory —

500 B.C. —

100 B.C. —

A.D. 100 —

200 —

500 —

1000 —

1200 —

1300 —

1400 —

1500 —

1600 —

1700 —

1800 —

1900 —

2000 —

2100 —

In about 3000 B.C., people in India began to grow cotton for making fabric. Like linen, cotton was lightweight and cool. Sometimes it was dyed various colors or stamped with decorative designs. Later, the use of cotton fabric for clothing spread to other areas, such as Europe and Africa. Some people called it "vegetable wool."

Humans who lived in ancient times were resourceful as well as creative. They taught themselves how to make fabric from plant and animal fibers, and they used the fabric to make whatever clothing they needed.

Fine Fabrics from India

People from India have produced vividly colored cotton fabrics for thousands of years. Today, the country produces about 6 billion yards of fabric annually, and more than half is still woven on hand looms. The patterns are often unique to the villages where they were created.

A nineteenth-century Chinese family sorts through silkworm cocoons, which produce strands that are woven into silk.

Artificial Silk

During the nineteenth century, many inventors experimented with chemicals to make silklike fabric. In the late 1800s, a Frenchman named Hilaire de Chardonnet spun fibers from cellulose, a substance derived from wood or cotton. By the 1920s, America's DuPont Corporation had secured the rights to use Chardonnet's formula. The company began producing a form of "artificial silk" known as rayon.

A Luxurious Fabric

While India's people were making fabric from cotton fibers, the Chinese learned to produce a soft, shimmering fabric called silk. The fabric was very different from flax, cotton, and wool because it did not come from plants or animals. Instead, it came from a unique type of worm.

According to ancient Chinese legend, the cocoon of a silkworm once fell from a mulberry tree and landed in an empress's teacup. She could see that long, delicate fibers had started to unravel from the cocoon. She also noticed many more cocoons in the tree. Later, the empress developed a technique for spinning the fine strands into thread. Then she wove the thread into fine, smooth silk cloth.

Once silk fabric had been created, many Chinese people began to raise silkworms. By 1500 B.C., they had developed intricate techniques for weaving silk threads that were dyed in a variety of colors. Women devoted a large part of

500 B.C. ——
100 B.C. ——
A.D. 100 ——
200 ——
500 ——
1000 ——
1200 ——
1300 ——
1400 ——
1500 ——
1600 ——
1700 ——
1800 ——
1900 ——
2000 ——
2100 ——

Silk-Making Creatures

A silkworm, which is about the size of an ant, can spin a cocoon in about a month. One silk fiber can be several thousand feet long, and it takes hundreds of cocoons (left) to make one silk shirt.

their days to raising silkworms. This included unraveling, spinning, and weaving the threads. They also dyed the silk fabric and embroidered it with unique designs. Chinese people used silk to create many garments, such as long, wide-sleeved robes.

For centuries, the Chinese hid their silk production methods from the rest of the world. It was a fiercely guarded secret—anyone caught trying to smuggle silkworms, cocoons, or eggs out of the country could be executed. Demand for the beautiful fabrics grew, and China regularly traded silk with other Asian countries, as well as Europe.

China continued to be the exclusive silk producer until about A.D. 500. Christian monks visiting China managed to smuggle silkworm eggs out of the country by hiding them in hollow walking sticks. For the first time, other countries were able to produce the lustrous fabric for themselves.

Chinese people used silk to make wide-sleeved silk garments, such as this child's coat from the 1800s.

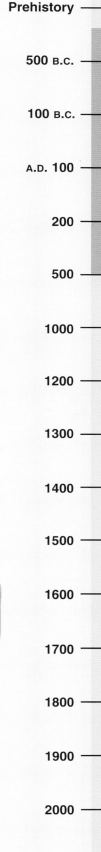

9

Clothing as a Status Symbol

The long, decorated silk robe of this Chinese emperor from around A.D. 1000 indicates his importance.

Silk was a highly desirable fabric because nothing was as luxurious. When people began to wear clothing that conveyed their social status, silk became even more prestigious. For instance, members of the elite classes in China wore long, decorative silk robes, while those of the lower class wore simple jackets and trousers. Starting about A.D. 1000, members of Chinese royalty wore robes embroidered with dragons.

In other countries, different types of fabric were used to make clothing for people of status. Kente cloth, for example, was created in West Africa during the twelfth century. Weavers used looms to make strips of fabric from an African palm known as raffia. Then they wove the strips together to create a variety of intricate textures and patterns. Originally, kente cloth was only used to make garments for kings and other members of royalty and high society.

In Egypt, women wore a formfitting dress known as the kalasiris. Some of the dresses

Japanese Custom

In Japan, the most common garments for women were flowing silk kimonos. However, kimonos with brightly colored flower patterns were considered suitable only for young, unmarried women.

Members of Chinese royalty wore clothing decorated with embroidered dragons. Peasants wore plain trousers and jackets.

This man in the West African country of Ghana weaves patterned kente cloth, which is made from the raffia plant.

fastened at the shoulder with straps, while others were strapless. Those worn by women of the upper class fell to the ankles. The garments were made of the finest linen, with pure gold thread woven throughout the fabric. These women often wore gold headbands as well as jewelry made from gold and precious stones. Women of the lower class also wore the kalasiris, but their garments were shorter and lacked any sort of decoration.

Greeks and Romans often wore loose garments known as togas, which were typically made of linen or wool. Togas were wrapped around the body and fastened at the shoulder. The longer and more elaborate they were, the higher the status of the people wearing them.

Unlike most ancient clothing, garments worn in the Middle Ages were more than just functional. People throughout the world dressed to convey messages about their wealth, status, and importance.

Made in Africa

The art of making kente cloth was developed centuries ago, but the fabric is still popular today. Most is made in the African country of Ghana, where skilled artists weave silk and cotton together to create unique and colorful fabrics.

Prehistory

500 B.C.

100 B.C.

A.D. 100

200

500

1000

1200

1300

1400

1500

1600

1700

1800

1900

2000

2100

11

Fastening Clothes Together

The togas and other garments people wore did not have fasteners like those on today's clothing. Instead, garments were usually tied at the shoulder or the waist. Some were fastened with long straight pins made out of thorns, bone, or wood. Another device that held clothes together was the fibula, a type of decorative fastener that resembles a brooch. Fibulae were often made of bronze, gold, or silver. Wealthy people decorated their clothing with ornamental fibulae that were adorned with precious stones.

Buttons originated thousands of years ago, but the earliest buttons were not used as fasteners. Instead, they were used to decorate clothing. In the thirteenth and fourteenth centuries, when European clothes became more formfitting, people started using buttons to fasten garments together. Buttons became so popular that clothing was often covered with them. European ladies dressed in garments with tight sleeves that were fastened with tiny buttons from the wrist to the elbow. Men often wore tunics that buttoned from the neck down to the hem.

To give the appearance of having a tiny waist, women wore tight corsets that often made breathing difficult.

The Zipper

Several inventors experimented with closing devices that could "zip" garments together. In 1917, Canadian engineer Gideon Sundback designed a "separable fastener" and received a patent for it. His fastener featured two rows of teeth and a sliding mechanism, and it later came to be known as the zipper.

During the 1500s, fancy buttons became a sign of social status and wealth. Some buttons were made of precious metals such as silver or gold and were often adorned with jewels. These early buttons had metal loops on the back called shanks, which were used to sew buttons onto clothing.

Beneath their formfitting dresses, many ladies wore corsets to mold their bodies into desired shapes. Corsets were fastened together with laces that tied in the front and back. Women tied the laces so tightly that they often had trouble breathing.

Just as garments in the sixteenth century were different from those worn today, fasteners were different as well. From laces and wooden pins to ornamental buttons, people used simple devices to hold their clothing together.

Sticky Fastener

In 1948, Swiss inventor George de Mestral went for a walk in the woods and returned home covered in burrs. He was fascinated with how the burrs stuck to his clothing, so he examined one under a microscope. He saw hundreds of tiny hooks that enabled the burr to stick to loops in fabric. Later, Mestral used that idea to invent a nylon fastener he called velcro, which was derived from the words velvet and crochet.

Magnified pictures show the similarities of the tiny hooks of a burr (inset) and velcro hooks (below). Burrs inspired the invention of velcro.

Prehistory —

500 B.C. —

100 B.C. —

A.D. 100 —

200 —

500 —

1000 —

1200 —

1300 —

1400 —

1500 —

1600 —

1700 —

1800 —

1900 —

2000 —

2100 —

Before Europeans arrived, Native Americans dressed in garments natural for the environment and climate, such as the loincloth worn by this Indian.

Clothing Crosses Cultures

The clothing styles worn in Europe during the 1600s began to appear in other parts of the world as well. Until European explorers settled in America, native peoples wore clothing that reflected their own unique cultures. They made clothing from cotton, palm leaf fibers, or bark. Men dressed in loincloths, with capes thrown over their bare chests. Sometimes they wore ceremonial warrior costumes and symbolized their status by wearing elaborate headdresses. Women typically wore wrapped skirts and blouses, although in some tribes they left their breasts bare. To the natives, this seminudity was natural and in keeping with their climate and environment.

The European settlers were shocked by how little clothing the native peoples wore. They considered it a sign of backwardness or savagery, and they influenced the natives to cover their bodies. Men began to wear pants instead of loincloths. They also wore long-sleeved shirts, and Spanish-style ponchos, and large straw or felt hats called sombreros, like those worn by men in Spain. Women began wearing Spanish-style garments as well, including long gathered skirts, tailored blouses, and lace scarves known as mantillas. Also, Spanish explorers introduced sheep to America. Afterward, native peoples began to weave much of their cloth out of wool rather than plant fibers.

Although native peoples throughout the world had dressed their own way for thousands of years, that began to change in the seventeenth century. Once the Europeans started exploring and conquering new lands, their way of life—including the clothing they wore—became a powerful instrument of change.

The Influence of Islam

In ancient times, many women in India left their breasts bare. However, when the Muslims invaded India, they spread the Islamic religion. Their holy book, the Koran, required people to cover themselves. As a result of Muslim rule, Indian women began wearing a type of blouse called the choli, which covered their breasts. Cholis were worn with skirts or under draped dresses called saris.

European exploration and settlement brought changes to the Indian way of life, including the way Indians dressed.

Prehistory ——

500 B.C. ——

100 B.C. ——

A.D. 100 ——

200 ——

500 ——

1000 ——

1200 ——

1300 ——

1400 ——

1500 ——

1600 ——

1700 ——

1800 ——

1900 ——

2000 ——

2100 ——

Making Fabric with Machines

As clothing styles continued to change throughout the world, fabric production was changing as well. Before the eighteenth century, spinning and weaving were done by hand, usually in people's homes. There were textile factories, but no automated equipment. Workers manually spun and wove fabrics. However, the Industrial Revolution transformed the way fabrics were made. This was a time of industrial growth that began in Europe during the mid-1700s, and then later spread to America. New machines were developed that enabled fabrics to be produced more quickly and inexpensively than ever before.

The Industrial Revolution introduced timesaving machines such as this loom from the 1880s, which sped up the production of fabrics.

One such machine was the flying shuttle, which partially automated the weaving process. Before the device was invented in 1733, weavers had to constantly push (or throw) a shuttle from side to side as the fibers were woven. This type of manual weaving was hard and time-consuming work. With the flying shuttle, a weaver just pushed a lever to throw the shuttle. The device saved enormous amounts of time—so much so that one worker could accomplish jobs that previously required two workers.

Soon, more machines were invented that further automated fabric production and sped up the process even more. The spinning jenny could spin eight times more thread or yarn than a traditional spinning wheel, because it used eight spindles instead of one. Later models had more than a hundred spindles. Another

People marvel at the demonstration of a power loom. Machines like this changed the way fabrics were made, and began the era of mass production.

invention, the power loom, made weaving faster and easier than ever before. Instead of being run by a weaver's hands and feet, the power loom was run by a steam engine.

These and other machines completely transformed the way fabrics were made. New mills and factories sprang up one by one, and they were filled with rows of fabric-making equipment. The era of mass production had been born, and the textile industry would never be the same.

The Cotton Gin

Prior to the Industrial Revolution, cleaning cotton was a tedious job. Tiny seeds clung to the cotton fibers and had to be pulled out by hand. The cotton gin, invented by Eli Whitney in the late 1700s, changed that. It simplified the cleaning of cotton by automatically separating the seeds from fibers. Because of the cotton gin, the production of cotton fabric skyrocketed.

Eli Whitney

Prehistory

500 B.C.

100 B.C.

A.D. 100

200

500

1000

1200

1300

1400

1500

1600

1700

1800

1900

2000

2100

Making Clothing with Machines

Even though machines were being used to produce fabric, clothing was still sewn by hand. There were small workshops where tailors and seamstresses worked together to sew garments, but most sewing was done in homes. Hand-tailored garments were expensive, so only well-to-do people could afford them.

By the mid-1800s, inventors were working on designs for machines that could sew. In 1830, a French tailor named Barthelemy Thimonnier designed the first working sewing machine. He opened a factory and began to sew uniforms for the French army. However, tailors were outraged about the invention because they feared it would put them out of work. Angry crowds destroyed his machines and burned the factory down. Thimonnier fled to England where he was granted a patent for his sewing machine. But, by that time other inventors had developed superior designs, and Thimonnier died nearly penniless.

One of the inventors was an American named Elias Howe. He introduced a machine in 1846 that was the first to sew with two separate threads. It used a lockstitch: A needle looped a thread from above with one from below. Later, Isaac Singer improved on Howe's design and invented a model with even better features.

A girl stitches clothes for her doll. Sewing in the early nineteenth century was done by hand, a time consuming process.

Prehistory ——

500 B.C. ——

100 B.C. ——

A.D. 100 ——

200 ——

500 ——

1000 ——

1200 ——

1300 ——

1400 ——

1500 ——

1600 ——

1700 ——

1800 ——

1900 ——

2000 ——

2100 ——

Futuristic Sewing

Elias Howe and Isaac Singer would not recognize today's sewing machines. The models of the 1800s that were operated by hand cranks or foot pedals have evolved into high-tech machines run by built-in computers. Programs for different stitches are stored in removable disks. Some sewing machines can even hook up to desktop computers and download patterns from the Internet.

Isaac Singer's sewing machine allowed for the mass production of garments, causing a boom in the clothing industry.

Singer's machine was operated by a foot pedal (called a treadle), whereas other machines used hand cranks. The treadle sewing machine began to appear in factories and homes throughout Europe and America. Clothing, like fabric, could now be mass-produced. By the end of the century, Singer had introduced a sewing machine that was powered by electricity. The price of garments dropped dramatically, and the clothing industry flourished. For the first time, people of average incomes could afford to buy ready-made clothes.

Of all the clothing-manufacturing machines ever invented, none was more important than the sewing machine. It simplified the chore of sewing garments and ushered in the era of ready-made clothing.

Before the invention of the washing machine, women had to wash clothing by hand, a long and tiring chore.

Keeping Clothes Clean

An Accidental Invention

It is commonly believed that dry cleaning was discovered by a Frenchman named Jean Baptiste Jolly. In the mid-1800s, he knocked over an oil lamp and accidentally spilled kerosene onto a tablecloth. When the fluid evaporated, a greasy stain disappeared with it. This motivated Jolly to experiment with different fluids and fabrics, and he developed a new process of cleaning clothes. He later opened the world's first dry cleaning establishment in Paris.

Another important invention of the late nineteenth century was the washing machine. Before it was invented, women washed their families' clothes by hand. Large washtubs were filled with water that was hand pumped from wells, since there was no such thing as running water. Then the garments were scrubbed on washboards—wooden boards with raised bumps. Most soap was made from lye, which was so harsh it often burned women's hands. After the scrubbing was done, clothes were rinsed in the washtub and put in baskets. Then the heavy baskets had to be carried outside, and the wet clothes had to be hung on clotheslines to dry in the sun. Washing clothes was a long, difficult, and tiring job.

In 1874, an Indiana man named William Blackstone wanted to make it easier for his wife to wash clothes. So he built her a washing machine as a birthday present. Inside a small wooden tub was a flat piece of wood with six wooden pegs. By turning a crank, Mrs. Blackstone swished clothes around in the tub in hot, soapy water. As the laundry snagged on the wooden pegs, the dirt was loosened (similar to the way a washboard worked). Soon, Blackstone began to build and sell his creations for $2.50 each.

Other inventors quickly came up with their own designs. Over the next decades, wooden tubs were replaced with metal tubs, and a wringer squeezed the water out of clothes. Hand cranks were eventually replaced with steam or gasoline engines. In 1906, the Hurley Machine Company of Chicago introduced the first washing machine that was powered by an electric motor.

From hand-held washboards to electric-powered washing machines, the process of keeping clothes clean became a much easier task in the nineteenth century.

The development of automated washing machines such as this one eased the task of cleaning clothes.

The washing machine in this advertisement features a wringer, which pressed the water from clothes.

Prehistory

500 B.C.

100 B.C.

A.D. 100

200

500

1000

1200

1300

1400

1500

1600

1700

1800

1900

2000

2100

Changes in China

For centuries, clothing in China was determined by social status, gender, and age. That began to change during the 1920s, when women began to dress in clothing that reflected Western styles. A slim dress with a high collar and slit skirt, known as the qi-pao, became popular. Also, for the first time in history, Chinese women began to wear silk stockings and high-heeled shoes.

Clothing Makes a Statement

By the early twentieth century, washing machines and other modern conveniences had radically changed women's lives. Tasks that had taken a full day to complete could now be done in a few hours, and this allowed women more freedom. Also, women's lives changed in other ways. During World War I, European and American men fought in the battlefields while women went to work in factories. After the war was over, women felt more independent. They fought for, and won, the right to vote in 1920. They wanted social and political restrictions on women removed. As their attitudes changed, their clothing changed as well.

As men left for World War I battlefields, American and European women began working in factories, which gave the women a feeling of independence.

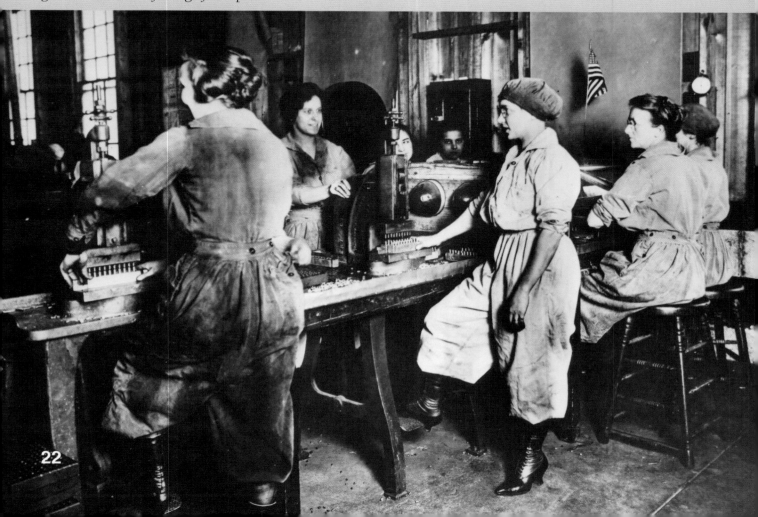

One major change was women's rejection of corsets. For centuries, they had worn the tight, confining undergarments to change the shapes of their bodies. However, during the 1920s, many protested the discomfort of corsets and stopped wearing them. Their dresses and blouses, which formerly had high collars, began to have lower, more revealing necklines.

Society was shocked at these radical changes in clothing, particularly at women's skirts—which were growing shorter. Never before had women in Western nations shown their legs. To do so was considered outrageous, even immoral. In the United States, some states even proposed laws that required women's skirts to reach the ankle. None were successful, though, and women continued to wear skirts that barely covered their knees.

Some American women, known as flappers, dressed in especially bold clothing. Unlike women of the past, flappers preferred boyish figures. To minimize their bustlines, they wound strips of fabric around their chests to flatten them. A flapper's typical attire included short skirts trimmed with fringe, brightly colored sweaters, and silk stockings. They cut their hair very short and wore felt hats known as cloches.

Women's clothing in the 1920s did not even resemble garments worn at the beginning of the century. As women became more independent, their clothing reflected their freedom.

Women's clothing in the 1920s, expressing newfound female independence, featured short skirts and low-cut blouses.

Prehistory

500 B.C.

100 B.C.

A.D. 100

200

500

1000

1200

1300

1400

1500

1600

1700

1800

1900

2000

2100

Clothing from Chemicals

As skirts continued to grow shorter, women became more conscious of their stockings. Most stockings in the 1920s were made of cotton. Silk stockings were also sold, but they were expensive. All but the wealthiest women reserved silk stockings for very special occasions.

During the 1930s, chemists began to experiment with chains of molecules called polymers, from which they created man-made fibers. They used the fibers to weave a synthetic fabric called nylon. DuPont Corporation used nylon to produce stockings that would be much cheaper to buy than those made from silk. At the 1939 World's Fair, DuPont introduced the stockings on the legs of female models. They were an immediate hit, and word of the amazing "miracle fiber" spread quickly. Women everywhere wanted to buy nylon stockings. However, two years after they were introduced, the stockings became unavailable. America had entered World War II, and nylon was reserved to make parachutes, tents, and other military equipment. After the war, nylon stockings became available again. Crowds of women mobbed stores to buy them.

This woman stitches nylon parachute harnesses during World War II. The military's demand for the synthetic material made nylon stockings unavailable to women.

This woman tries on her new nylon stockings after being first in a postwar line to purchase the popular items.

The success of nylon led to the creation of other synthetic fabrics. During the 1940s, scientists created a fiber called Orlon. In 1952, DuPont introduced it as a replacement for wool. Many people preferred Orlon sweaters because they did not itch like wool and did not shrink when they were washed.

Another fabric made from chemicals was spandex, which was introduced in 1959. Soon, spandex began to replace heavy rubber in brassieres and other undergarments. Rubber was heavy and uncomfortable and could stretch out of shape. Spandex, however, could stretch to five times its length and then snap back to its original form.

In just two decades, fabrics made from chemicals became as common as those from natural fibers. From nylon stockings to Orlon sweaters, synthetic fibers changed clothing dramatically.

Artificial Rubber

In 1931, DuPont introduced neoprene, a man-made substitute for rubber. Today, neoprene is used to make wet suits, fishing waders, and gloves, as well as many other types of specialty clothing.

Prehistory

500 B.C.

100 B.C.

A.D. 100

200

500

1000

1200

1300

1400

1500

1600

1700

1800

1900

2000

2100

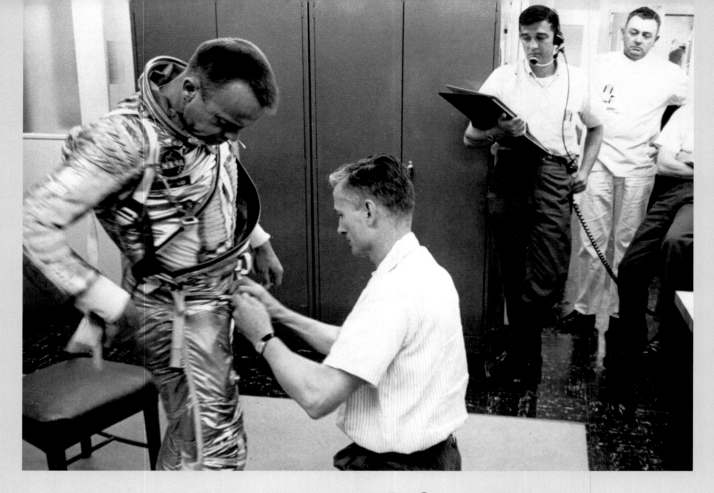

Astronaut Alan Shepard gets fitted with a protective space suit in 1961. The astronauts of the Apollo missions required much more advanced space suits.

Suited for Space

The invention of synthetic fibers was an important breakthrough for the clothing industry. The fibers were used to make everyday clothing, as well as special kinds of suits—those worn by astronauts. Spaceships climbed thousands of miles above the earth, where it was very cold and there was no oxygen. Even though astronauts did not leave the spacecraft during early missions, their suits had to protect them while they were inside.

The first space suits, designed in 1959, were for Project Mercury. The suits had an inner layer of nylon fabric that was coated with a man-made rubber substitute called neoprene, and an air hose was attached. If the spacecraft cabin suddenly lost pressure, air would blow through the hose and inflate the suit around the astronaut's body. The outer layer of the suit was made of strong nylon. The Mercury astronauts also wore protective helmets, boots, and gloves.

The 1969 Apollo mission gave astronauts their first chance to walk on the moon. For this, a much more elaborate space suit was required. Because the astronauts would bend and stoop as they picked up lunar rocks, their space suits needed to be flexible. Also, billions of tiny rocks known as micrometeoroids constantly pelt the moon's surface. To protect the astronauts, the space suits had outer layers of material made from glass fibers. Helmets protected the astronauts' heads, while boots and gloves protected their feet and hands. Beneath their space suits, astronauts wore undergarments designed to keep their bodies cool when daytime temperatures grew scorching hot. The garment looked similar to a pair of long underwear. It had a network of spaghettilike tubing sewn onto the fabric. Cool water continuously circulated through the tubing to keep the astronauts comfortable.

The space suits designed in the 1960s were like no clothing before them. They had to be comfortable and flexible, but most importantly, they needed to protect astronauts against the hazards of space travel.

Survival on the Red Planet

Scientists are now working on a space suit that is different from anything that has ever been developed. It is being designed for astronauts who will one day travel to the planet Mars, a mission NASA plans for sometime after 2020. The space suits must be built to protect astronauts against conditions more hostile than anyone has ever encountered in space. Also, they must be very comfortable. Astronauts will live and work in the suits for many hours each day—and their stay on Mars will last for up to three years.

Astronauts explore Mars in this illustration. Scientists are developing space suits able to withstand the extreme conditions of the Martian environment.

Prehistory ——

500 B.C. ——

100 B.C. ——

A.D. 100 ——

200 ——

500 ——

1000 ——

1200 ——

1300 ——

1400 ——

1500 ——

1600 ——

1700 ——

1800 ——

1900 ——

2000 ——

2100 ——

Breathing Vest

The Avalung is a high-tech vest that was designed to protect mountain climbers and skiers in the event of an avalanche. Most people who perish in avalanches die because they suffocate. The Avalung can help prevent suffocation because it has a pipe attached that allows someone to breathe—even if he or she is completely buried under snow.

High-Tech Wear

Space suits have always been designed to protect astronauts from hazards in space. Today, there are many garments specially made to protect people from hazards on this planet—and some use materials that are used on space missions. For instance, suits worn by racing-car drivers have collars lined with the same heavy-duty foam that NASA uses in spacecraft seats. The foam protects a driver's neck in the event of an accident. The collars also protect drivers from the extreme heat caused by fiery crashes. DuPont's Nomex, a synthetic material that helps control body temperatures in space suits, is also used in racing suits. The material cannot burn or melt, and it

Synthetic materials help save lives. This firefighter wears a protective suit made of Nomex, which does not melt or burn.

reflects heat, so it provides protection from fires. In addition to suits, Nomex is also used in driving gloves, socks, shoes, and underwear.

Nomex is not limited to suits for race car drivers. Firefighters also wear protective suits made from Nomex, as do some police officers. For instance, law enforcement helicopter crews in Tampa, Florida, wear navy blue Nomex flight suits. The garments could save the officers' lives in the event of a helicopter crash.

Another synthetic material that is essential for police officers and soldiers in combat zones is DuPont's Kevlar. Ounce for ounce, Kevlar is five times stronger than steel, so it acts like body armor. One use for the material is in bulletproof vests. When a bullet strikes a Kevlar vest, it is caught in a web of strong fibers. The fibers absorb and spread the energy of the impact. The bullet "mushrooms" and is then trapped within multiple layers of Kevlar. As a result, it cannot penetrate the vest, although the shock from the impact can cause some nasty bruises.

From Nomex to Kevlar, garments made from high-tech synthetic materials are invaluable. They can mean the difference between life and death for people who wear them.

A handler outfits this police dog with a bulletproof vest made of Kevlar, a material five times stronger than steel.

Fabrics Made from Mirrors?

A team of scientists has created mirrors that can be formed into hair-thin fibers and then woven into fabrics. Using this technology, garments could be created that reflect and protect against invisible microwaves and harmful radiation.

Prehistory

500 B.C.

100 B.C.

A.D. 100

200

500

1000

1200

1300

1400

1500

1600

1700

1800

1900

2000

2100

Today most people in the world wear Western-style clothing for everyday life, but often dress in traditional garments on special occasions.

Clothing Today

Clothing has come a long way over the years. What began as animal skins and plant fibers has evolved into garments that are strong enough to protect people's lives. Today, clothing worn by most people throughout the world is influenced by Western culture. However, there are many countries where clothing reflects cultural traditions and religion.

In Japan, for instance, people typically wear the same styles of dresses, suits, and even blue jeans that are worn by people in Europe and America. But for special occasions, many Japanese men and women still wear traditional silk kimonos. In India, some women dress in Western-style garments, although most prefer to wear saris. The flowing garments are made of cotton, silk, or synthetic materials. Underneath the saris women wear petticoats, which are floor-length skirts that tie tightly at the waist with a drawstring.

Not Everyone Wears Clothing

In remote jungles throughout the world, there are still many people whose custom is to wear no clothes. For instance, the Amazon rain forest in Brazil is home to numerous tribes, one of which is the Awa Guaja. The males of the tribe go naked except for headbands of bright orange plumage made from toucan feathers. The men also wear armbands made from the feathers of yellow and red macaws.

In Muslim countries, where people practice the religion of Islam, there is a strong emphasis on modesty. Garments must not be thin enough to see through, and clothing must hang loosely so the shape of someone's body is not obvious. In some Muslim countries, women still wear head-to-toe garments called burkas.

After years of choosing synthetic fabrics such as polyester, many Americans began preferring natural fibers such as cotton, linen, and silk. However, man-made fibers continue to be perfected. Some synthetic garments look nearly identical to those made from natural fibers, so the popularity of synthetic fabrics is once again on the rise.

Today's clothing serves many functions. It can provide protection from the elements or be fashionable. Some garments save lives, while others communicate religious beliefs. Clothing may be made of silk, cotton, Kevlar, or polyester. It may copy Western styles, or reflect traditional cultures. Throughout the ages, clothing has been as varied as the people who wear it—and that is still true today.

The Muslim religion requires women to dress modestly. Some Muslim women cover themselves completely.

Prehistory ——

500 B.C. ——

100 B.C. ——

A.D. 100 ——

200 ——

500 ——

1000 ——

1200 ——

1300 ——

1400 ——

1500 ——

1600 ——

1700 ——

1800 ——

1900 ——

2000 ——

2100 ——

Glossary

anthropologist: A scientist who specializes in the history of humans.

cellulose: A material derived from living plants.

fibula: A decorative fastener used by ancient peoples.

flax: A flowering plant from which fibers are obtained to make linen.

Industrial Revolution: A period of rapid industrial growth in Europe and America that began in the mid-eighteenth century.

kalasiris: A garment worn by people in ancient Egypt.

kente cloth: A special type of woven cloth that originated in West Africa.

Koran: The holy book of people (called Muslims) who practice the Islamic religion.

loom: A device or machine used to weave fabrics.

micrometeoroid: Tiny fragments of rock that hurtle through space.

polymers: Compounds of molecules that are used to make synthetic fabrics.

For More Information

Books

Erhard Klepper, *Costume Through the Ages*. Mineola, NY: Dover, 1999.

Fiona MacDonald, *Clothing and Jewelry*. New York: Crabtree, 2001.

John Peacock, *The Chronicle of Western Fashion*. New York: Harry N. Abrams, 1991.

Internet Sources

Microsoft Encarta Online Encyclopedia 2004, "Clothing" (http://encarta.msn.com/encyclopedia_761569657/Clothing .html). An excellent, in-depth article about the history of clothing, the functions of clothing, and different types of garments worn by people around the world.

National Aeronautics and Space Administration (NASA), "Space Suits on Parade" (http://media.nasaexplores.com lessons/02-028/fullarticle.pdf). An interesting article about space suits worn on the various space missions.

Web Sites

About.com: Inventors (http://inventors.about.com/cs/ inventorsalphabet/a/toc.htm). Includes a good collection information about the Industrial Revolution, including th many inventions and their effects on textile production.

History for Kids: Europe, Asia, and Africa Before 1500 AD (www.historyforkids.org/learn/clothing). An interesting collection of information about how people lived in ancient times, with a special section on how clothing was made.

Index